# The Lord of the Dance

## Understanding the Secret of the Stairs

Rebecca Park Totilo

The Lord of the Dance

Published by Rebecca at the Well Foundation, PO Box 60044, St. Petersburg, Florida 33784.

Scripture references are taken from the King James Version of the Bible.

ISBN 978-0-9749115-5-7

# Acknowledgments

First, I would like to extend my deepest gratitude to Wade E. Taylor for his revelation into the secret of the stairs that leads us into spiritual maturity as the Bride of Messiah. Some of his insights included in this work were taken from his book entitled, "Secret of the Stairs." I highly recommend every believer read this book. It will change your life.

Second, I would like to thank C.R. Oliver, for his insightful book, "Solomon's Secret." Those seeking to know their Heavenly Bridegroom more intimately will find this commentary on the Song of Solomon to be like discovering a hidden jewel.

And, finally to Barbara Urban, author of "Dance of the Shulamite:" Your passion and zeal leapt off the pages sending my soul soaring toward Heaven. Your work is greatly appreciated and once again, I highly recommend her book to those who consider themselves the "Shulamite."

# Table of Contents

# Your Bridal Dance

In an adorable movie entitled, "Little Colonel," starring Shirley Temple and Bill "Bo Jangles" Robinson, a family illness causes Shirley to have to spend the night at her crotchety old grandfather's southern plantation. Reluctant to go to bed, Mr. Robinson, a household servant, persuades her by promising to teach her a new way to go up the stairs. In this extraordinary performance, both tap dance there way up and down the stairs like angels.

This scene reminds me of how we act toward God. I too, have behaved like this little girl, standing at the foot of the stairs next to our Heavenly Father, stubbornly not wanting to take His hand and allow Him to lead me up to the next level. This stubbornness in me demonstrated an unwillingness to let God be in control of my life. We all want to ascend into spiritual maturity, but do we trust Him enough to let Him take the lead and teach us a new way in developing that relationship we all desire?

In Barbara Urban's book, "The Dance of the Shulamite," she writes:

"The dance of unbridled passion for the Son of God, is expressed in extravagant acts of unwavering obedience. We all have a dance in us. That dance is an expression of God within us, complimenting His kingdom. Unfortunately, many dance to the captivating sound of the prince and power of the air, while others are enslaved to the primal dance of their own carnality. Some even become ensnared by the dance of religion, chained to legalistic maneuvers which keep them far from the heart of the Father. But there are a few who actually hear the love call of the Beloved. They are the ones who break out of the confines of this life and live a life of the kingdom here and now, and dance a prophetic dance of passionate love and tenacious obedience. That is the dance of the Shulamite."

As you will discover, our bridal dance as believers is one of incomparable devotion toward our Heavenly Bridegroom. Penned within Solomon's Song is this extravagant love affair between the Shulamite, her Beloved—and all who share a passion for the King of Kings. In this prophetic work, we will discover how the Bride learns to trust her dance partner, Yeshua and follow His lead in this Heavenly waltz up the stairs into His chambers.

Our dance with our Beloved proclaims who we are, what we believe and the truth we now embrace. Author, Jane Clark calls this bridal dance a "full expression of the soul in movement." But, how do we know if we are dancing His Dance?

"It is genuinely impossible to dance another's dance. In fact, the imitation of another's dance or passion for God will hinder the release of your own dance. Our Bridegroom desires your dance to be one that is distinctly you, placed deep within your spirit by the Creator. It cannot be learned or choreographed—it is birthed within you," Urban describes in her book. It is one of restoration—beauty on display for our King.

In this study, you will become more familiar with the necessary steps to help you move past the veil of redemption into the realm of intimacy, developing a deeper passion for our Beloved Bridegroom.

# *Learning the Dance Steps*

The Lord of the Dance desires to usher each of us into a new level of spiritual maturity with him. Yet, the matter in which he chooses to reveal these moves are not plainly written for the casual believer to observe. They are hidden within the pages of the Song of Solomon in the life of the Shulamite. Her journey is our journey—those who are part of the remnant bride and desire to know him more intimately. These principles can only be discovered by those who diligently and prayerfully seek him, applying them to their life. As we acquaint ourselves with his desires and learn to obey our Beloved's voice, our commitment to His ways deepens and thus, we begin the ascent up the stairs.

The opening scene of Solomon 1:2 demonstrates the bride's response to His Song of Love as she cries for intimate communion with Him, "Let Him kiss me with the kisses of His mouth: for Thy love is better than wine." She expresses her heart plainly as one that is completely in love and surrendered to the lover of her soul. Once you have been kissed this way, nothing else will suffice. Yet, while He is the initiator of this kiss, she invites Him to kiss her with all of his kisses—unlike the Israelites who asked Yahweh to speak only to Moses. And, because of their refusal to share in an intimate relationship, they were left with only commandments written on stone and a tabernacle. In this song though, the bride is receptive to Him and gladly embraces all that He has to offer. She knows Him intimately now, not just "about Him" or "His ways."

As you embrace your Heavenly Dance Partner, lean upon his chest like John the beloved disciple did and listen to His heartbeat. He is the author of forgiveness and tender love. C.R. Oliver, author of "Solomon's Secret" states it so beautifully:

"He established Love to rule over Law. Those who understood Him in this matter broke bottles of ointment and bathed His feet, toweling them with their hair. Those who did not understand this entreated Him with doctrinal statements and dilemmas of religion. The same is true today! Those who do not understand Him choose, like Judas, to kiss Him rather than be kissed by Him."

The Lord of the Dance

Like a ballerina learning to stand up on tip toes, we must master the balance between grace and Law. While we have a newfound freedom and liberty in Messiah, we must continue to walk in obedience to His commands. Yeshua said in John 14:15, "If ye love me, keep my commandments." One of the most obvious ways to demonstrate your love to the Lord is to do what He says. Ask Him in prayer to reveal anything that may hinder you from entering into a deeper spiritual realm with Him. If the Lord reveals anything to you, confess it as sin and allow Him to cleanse your heart. Once He sees your desire is for Him more than anything else, He will gently begin to guide you toward the entrance to the stairs that will lead you upward into His chambers.

# *Following His Lead*

Sometimes we tend to focus on our shortcomings and the negative instead of the positive. In fact, we don't see much spiritual growth in ourselves at all! Our testimony and confession tends to reveal our spiritual condition. In Song of Solomon 1:5-6 the Shulamite explains:

> "I am black, but comely, O ye daughters of Jerusalem, as the tents of Kedar, as the curtains of Solomon. Look not upon me, because I am black, because the sun hath looked upon me: my mother's children were angry with me; they made me the keeper of the vineyards; but mine own vineyard have I not kept."

The Shulamite confesses to the daughters of Jerusalem why she lacks spiritual growth—she has not kept her own vineyard because of taking care of other's spiritual needs. While her life has been centered around the vine—a picture of Yeshua, as He is the true vine, she has labored hard in the heat of the day for those in the body (mother's children).

With all the business of meetings and ministry, we cannot allow this to replace our time with the Lord. Just as the Shulamite realizes her actions cannot replace her time with Him, nor can we neglect our relationship with Yah. We must remain connected to Him, as we are the branches and He is the vine, in which we draw strength and nourishment from. We all desire to flourish with zeal and life, which is why it is sometimes difficult to say "no" to another meeting or special cause. The Shulamite explains it as her "mother's children" being angry with her. Others may not understand your reason for solitude or God's calling you to be set apart, but in many cases the Lord uses occasions like these to provoke feelings of uneasiness and restlessness to gently nudge us away from those we have become "spiritually dependent" upon. The Lord desires to draw you up the stairs to His secret chambers.

With intense desire, the Shulamite longs to know what she should do, and asks the Lord for guidance in Song of Solomon 1:7:

The Lord of the Dance

"Tell me, O Thou Whom my soul loveth,
where Thou feedest, where Thou makest
Thy flock to rest at noon: for why should I
be as one that turneth aside by the flocks of
Thy companions?"

In her busyness, she had become self-reliant. The Shulamite felt deep within her a longing for more. She desired to hear His voice again, to be near Him.

Here she is asking, "Where are those that truly dance with you?" She wanted to find His manifest presence and those that share the same revelation she has of Him.

The Shulamite didn't want to be misled again by forms of religion. Neither did she want the rehashed second-hand interpretation of Scripture. She wanted to hear directly from Yeshua herself.

We too, cannot afford to be satisfied with another's testimony or interpretation of the Word—no one else can satisfy this deep need in the heart of His bride.

He instructs her to search out those who truly know Him. In Song of Solomon 1:8 he answers:

"If thou know not, O thou fairest among women, go thy way forth by the footsteps of the flock, and feed thy kids beside the shepherds' tents."

He suggests to her to follow after the footsteps of the flock—those of kindred-spirit. These are those that have an understanding of His ways and Torah. They will lead her to Him—these are the footstep patterns we all have before us. The Scriptures refer to these as "old paths" in Jeremiah 6:16, it reads:

"Thus saith the LORD, Stand ye in the ways, and see, and ask for the old paths, where is the good way, and walk therein, and ye shall find rest for your souls…"

As the remnant bride, it is our intense spiritual desire that causes Him to turn aside from others or those of the House of Judah (daughters of Jerusalem) to pursue us as His potential bride. Our passionate desire toward Him causes Him to turn all of His attention toward us. His answer tells us we should seek out those who are truly following Him. God chooses to reveal His glory through men and women and says, "Now that you can tell the truth from lies, seek out those who are speaking My truth."

The Lord is not suggesting we become the center of attention in this dance. He is still in the business of building a company. He points her to those who have gone before her on this journey and know the dance steps that can help teach her His glorious moves living a life that observe His commands victoriously.

# *The Chorus Line*

We read in Song of Solomon 1:9, "I have compared thee, O my love, to a company of horses in Pharaoh's chariots." The Geneva Study Bible's commentary describes this verse in this way: "For your spiritual beauty and excellency there was no worldly treasure to be compared to you." What an amazing comparison of untapped power and potential He sees in her!

Pharaoh's agents were sent throughout the known world to seek immature ponies (he had 70,000 horses hand-picked in his army) to be hitched to his magnificent gold-overlaid chariot. After intense training and discipline, the horses that qualified were chosen to pull his chariot. In a beautiful demonstration of beauty, swiftness and unity, they ushered in the king in all his regal glory.

Interestingly, the horses brought at a high price by Solomon were out of Egypt (2 Ch. 1:16, 17), just as the bride is redeemed out of spiritual Egypt by the true Solomon, Yeshua, at an infinite price (1 Peter 1:18-19).

The Lord sees these same qualities in you and believes you demonstrate the traits necessary to effectively respond to His training and discipline. Are you are willing to submit yourself as a living sacrifice, a calling that requires your giving all—body, soul, and spirit in order to allow the Word to be made flesh? You can be a part of this company, in Hebrew meaning *Machaneh*, an "army of dancers." In ranks, this host will usher in the King of Kings in all His beauty, majesty, and splendor at the second coming.

# Finding Your Own Style

Your blend of proficiency, skill and dexterity exhibited in your worship and lifestyle is an upward path of stairs. Song of Solomon 2:14 says,

> "O my dove, that art in the clefts of the rock, in the secret places of the stairs, let me see thy countenance, let me hear thy voice; for sweet is thy voice, and thy countenance is comely."

These words are actually those of the Bridegroom speaking to His bride. The Hebrew word for "secret" is *Cether*, which means covering, shelter, or hiding place. He has opened His heart to her and she now abides in the shadow of the almighty under His protection. But, He has much more for His bride. He doesn't want her to remain at the bottom of the stairs hidden, but to ascend higher in Him. The Lord wants to hear her speak— "for thy voice is sweet."

The Lord's heart toward you is "let me hear" your voice — an expression of His desire to see you dance before Him as David sang and danced in worship before the Lord. In 2 Samuel 6:14 it says, "Then David danced before the Lord with all his might; and David was wearing a linen ephod (priestly garments)."

In Song of Solomon 1:12 we see the Shulamite lift up her voice in worship to the King. She says, "While the king sitteth at his table, my spikenard sendeth forth the smell thereof."

Spikenard is a costly spice which comes from a very rare plant usually blended with olive oil for anointing acts of consecration, dedication, and worship. Her statement is quite prophetic, speaking yet of another King—the King of Kings.

In Greek, the word for "spikenard" means "genuine and pure." In John 12:3, the Bible tells how spikenard was used to anoint Yeshua, the pure and spotless Lamb, just days before His death and burial:

"Then Mary took a pound of ointment of spikenard, very costly, and anointed the feet of Jesus, and wiped his feet with her hair: and the house was filled with the odor of the ointment."

Mark 14:3 tells us of another woman who came, having an alabaster flask of very precious oil of spikenard. After she broke the seal and poured the oil on Yeshua's head, some of the disciples were very indignant with the "waste" of costly oil, as it may have cost this woman as much as a whole year's wages. But Yeshua rebuked them and said she had done a good work, for He knew His life would soon be broken, just like the alabaster jar filled with the costly scent. Not a drop of her extravagant act of worship was wasted in His eyes. Yeshua said her deed would be remembered wherever the Gospel would be preached.

Whisper words of adoration—shout praises to His name—for every swirl in dance, bowed knee in prayer or shout from the hilltop reaches His throne. Worship extravagantly! Let the Lord hear your voice in worship toward Him with a pure, genuine heart of devotion. Our fragrance is our love and dedication to Him—and He will take notice of it. This is all we have to offer as worship to the King.

In Song of Solomon 2:14, the king asks her to "let me see," an expression to determine her willingness to obey

Him and come into His presence. In Wade E. Taylor's book, "Secret of the Stairs," he says, "Our response in this will determine the action the Lord will take to bring us into the full fruition of the potential He sees within us."

How will you respond to the Lord? Will you be like Mary, the mother of Yeshua, who unconditionally yielded to the Holy Spirit and replied, "Behold, the maidservant of the Lord, let it be unto me according to your word." Or, behave like Vashti who flatly refused to obey the King's request to "show off her beauty?"

The Hebrew word for "see" is *Ra'ah*, which means to inspect, perceive, consider, learn about, observe, watch, give attention to, gaze at, or to look at each other's face. The Lord desires to inspect or observe your countenance. Our countenance reveals the true condition of the heart. While we try to conceal flaws, the truth is, our countenance always tells what's going on in the inside.

While learning a new routine takes practice, you will soon be moving with grace and elegance. The secret to learning these dance steps will be made known to you as you submit to His will.

# *One Step at a Time*

In Taylor's book, he explains that as you respond to the Lord and begin to climb the stairs, you must consider that a "stair" has first a riser and then a step, or platform. He writes:

> "The first riser and step may be called "revelation." When a scripture is quickened within me, my understanding is "opened" concerning it. As I embrace this understanding (the riser) and act upon it (the step), it will become a personal reality within my life experience."

We all have experienced this at some point in our walk with the Lord. A Bible verse pops out at you. It may have been one in which you have read many times, but this time it comes alive in a new way. This is the revelation He is showing you. Now, you must walk in this truth that has been revealed to you. James 1:22 tells us, "But be ye doers of the word, and not hearers only, deceiving your own selves." This is a call to action. God's desire is to teach us, but He wants us to act upon His Word and apply it to our life, so change will take place. This will give you the "living testimony" that no one can challenge. Once you have experienced revelation knowledge, this will bring you to the next riser and step in your spiritual growth. Our ascent toward the Lord will progress one step at a time.

Taylor explains, "The first riser and step is called "revelation." When a scripture is quickened within you, your understanding is opened concerning it. As you embrace this truth (riser), and act upon it (step), it will become a personal reality within your life experience—a testimony that no one can take from you."

On Arthur Murray Studio's website (www.arthurmurray.com) I found the following steps in learning how to dance. It is amazingly similar to what a believer experiences in learning how to observe the Torah and mature as a believer.

1. THE INITIAL LEARNING STAGE

The student is introduced to the skill or step.

## 2. THE AWKWARD USE STAGE

The student has an increased awareness, but feels awkward and frequently experiences difficulty.

## 3. THE CONSCIOUS USE STAGE

The student is able to do the skill or step more effectively and easily; however, even though the task may look good, it must still be thought through when performed.

## 4. THE NATURAL USE STAGE

This skill or step is done with ease and is spontaneous, comfortable and creative. This level is reached only after a period of time in which the student has continued to use and practice the skill.

*Every time you learn something new, your body will always go through the Stages of Learning. It is natural for you to progress through these stages.*

# Dance Rehearsals

The Lord will schedule "dance rehearsals" or a "set of circumstances to bring you into a practical understanding (learning) of this new spiritual reality," Taylor says. Divine opportunities will be presented to you, as the Lord waits and watches to see how you will respond. Your willing response will ascend to the next riser and step in the process of your spiritual growth, ever toward His chambers. The revelation that you receive (riser) will become a part of you and reflect Yeshua in your daily walk. This will be something that is reflected in your lifestyle.

One example of this is when the Lord challenged me to change my diet and eat only Biblical "clean" foods. Having been raised in the south where every meal included something from the category of "unclean" non-foods such as pork and shellfish, this was a real challenge. It felt very unnatural and required a great effort on my part to find new recipes. Grocery shopping took twice as long in checking labels and asking the deli department to clean their machines before slicing my turkey or roast beef. "To be careful to observe His law" took on a whole new meaning. But with obedience, the Lord began to reveal many deep spiritual truths regarding the "clean" and "unclean." Since changing my diet, I have developed an incredible ability for the discernment of spirits. The Word of God is much richer as spiritual food as well. I also believe that my act of obedience broke a curse of heart disease on my family tree.

Many may not share my conviction to follow Levitical law in eating Biblically Kosher. That is the beauty of the secret of the stairs. The Lord may have you in a different place in your journey and spiritual growth process. We are all on different levels, ascending and descending like angels on Jacob's ladder. He may be dealing with you regarding something totally different like trusting Him in finances, or an attitude of the heart concerning a co-worker. As we die to ourselves and our own way, He will release us to move into circumstances He has prearranged on the level we are at.

As the spirit of obedience is birthed and strengthened through these progressive steps we take toward Him, each step will become an abiding reality and strength within us.

# *Listening to our Instructor*

It is hard to imagine our Lord and Savior as a young boy sitting on the courtyard steps of the Temple listening and asking questions to the Rabbis of His day. Luke 2:46-47 records this brief account of His childhood:

> "And it came to pass, that after three days they found him in the temple, sitting in the midst of the doctors, both hearing them, and asking them questions. And all that heard him were astonished at his understanding and answers. And when they saw him, they were amazed: and his mother said unto him, Son, why hast thou thus dealt with us? behold, thy father and I have sought thee sorrowing. And he said unto them, How is it that ye sought me? wist ye not that I must be about my Father's business? And they understood not the saying which he spake unto them. And he went down with them, and

came to Nazareth, and was subject unto
them: but his mother kept all these sayings
in her heart."

At an early age, Yeshua was about His Father's business; that is, studying the Torah to show Himself approved.
He also submitted Himself to His earthly parents. In doing
so, He gained favor with God and man. Later in life, He
submitted Himself to the temptations and trials of the
wilderness, proving Himself that while being fully man (Phil.
2:6-7), He was able to resist the temptation of doing His
own will, and subject Himself only to that which was the
Father's will. We see in Scripture how Yeshua learned
obedience. Hebrews 5:8-9 says:

"Though he were a Son, yet learned he obedience by the things which he suffered; and
being made perfect, he became the author of
eternal salvation unto all them that obey
him."

Yeshua qualified Himself to become the author of
our salvation, not just because it was the will of God for
Him, but He qualified Himself through His life experiences

to become Savior of the World. As Taylor puts it, "The word needed to be fully experienced and made flesh."

Much in the same way, our Heavenly Father, author Wade E. Taylor writes, "Will cause the "letter" of the Law that has been written on the tablets of our heart, to become "experientially" a part of us. This is a spiritual law— that the truth is never ours until we have experienced it and it has become a part of us. The two of these: spiritual experience coupled with the Word will become alive and so real within us that we will see Yeshua at the center of it and know Him as never before."

Many times when believers are in a trial, they seek to be immediately relieved from that time of testing. "Where is God?" they ask. In the case of Job, he voiced his complaint to God in Job 23:1-10:

> "Even to day is my complaint bitter: my stroke is heavier than my groaning. Oh that I knew where I might find him! that I might come even to his seat! I would order my cause before him, and fill my mouth with arguments. I would know the words which he would answer me, and understand what he

would say unto me. Will he plead against me with his great power? No; but he would put strength in me. There the righteous might dispute with him; so should I be delivered for ever from my judge. Behold, I go forward, but he is not there; and backward, but I cannot perceive him: On the left hand, where he doth work, but I cannot behold him: he hideth himself on the right hand, that I cannot see him: But he knoweth the way that I take: when he hath tried me, I shall come forth as gold."

Job's final conclusion regarding his complaint before God was "when I am finished." God will deliver you when He is finished perfecting your faith. The Lord is determined to do a complete work in the heart of His bride. For when you are tried, you shall come forth as gold in the image and likeness of our Savior. His bride is all fair, there is no spot found in her (SS 4:7).

These experiences will give you the opportunity to identify with the Lord in the fellowship of His sufferings, while being involved in the outworking of His purposes. As you ascend to each new level, your revelation and experience will be tested and proven. Philippians 3:10 tells us:

> "That I may know him, and the power of his resurrection, and the fellowship of his sufferings, being conformable unto his death."

Take hold of your Heavenly Dance Instructor as He leads you through these trials and testing, so that you can be changed into the bride that He desires. His desire is that we embrace His sufferings, not just suffer through them. All believers must be willing for this process to take place in order to be the bride. Those who do will find the spiritual rewards to be "exceeding abundantly above all that we ask or think (Eph. 3:20)" as a result of your willing obedience to Him.

# In the Dark Hours

Most know what it is like to have a "wilderness experience"—everything in your prayer life and bible reading seems dry and barren. You may wonder where God is, just as the Shulamite did in Song of Solomon 3:1: "By night on my bed I sought him whom my soul loveth: I sought him, but I found him not."

During these dark night hours we feel forgotten and lifeless. But spiritually, it is like a seed buried in the ground, waiting to sprout. God's Word promises the wilderness and desert will again bloom. Isaiah 35:1-4 tells us:

> "The wilderness and the solitary place shall be glad for them; and the desert shall rejoice, and blossom as the rose. It shall blossom abundantly, and rejoice even with joy and singing: the glory of Lebanon shall be given unto it, the excellency of Carmel and Sharon, they shall see the glory of the LORD, and

the excellency of our God. Strengthen ye the weak hands, and confirm the feeble knees. Say to them that are of a fearful heart, Be strong, fear not: behold, your God will come with vengeance, even God with a recompence; he will come and save you."

He is slowly transforming us into a blossoming garden, consecrated for His purposes. Song of Solomon 6:2 tells us, "My beloved is gone down into his garden, to the beds of spices, to feed in the gardens, and to gather lilies."

We are no longer barren and lifeless—we are a garden for Him, and for His enjoyment. The sweet savor and fragrance of our garden draws others, like the butterflies and bees drawn to fragrant flowers. And, once our garden truly becomes His garden, we proclaim: "Awake, O north wind; and come, thou south; blow upon my garden, that the spices thereof may flow out" (SS 4:16). The swirling winds of the north that blow can be harsh, filled with affliction, or warm, gentle summer breezes of refreshment—both emit His fragrance. In this, He is not only embracing us, we are embracing Him.

Earlier in the Shulamite's journey in Song of Solomon 2:5 she cried, "Stay me with flagons, comfort me with apples: for I am sick of love" and how "she sat down under His shadow with great delight, and His fruit was sweet to my taste" (SS 2:3). The Shulamite had taken delight in His fruit and partook of all His wonderful blessings. She came to a place of satisfaction and found rest and comfort abiding in His shadow. Suddenly, the bride finds herself all alone, no longer feasting at His banqueting table. The Lord had met all her needs and she was satisfied with his physical provisions. What she didn't realize was there was so much more for her besides just fulfilling her physical needs. Now she finds herself seeking Him where He is not. And her own fruitless efforts leave her tossing in bed.

He had declared His love and in anticipation, awaited her response to see if she desired His companionship too. In Song of Solomon 2:13 He declared, "Arise, My love, My fair one, and come away." Now in Song of Solomon 3:1, it is apparent she had refused His invitation to come away. A decision all believers must make—whether to accept His invitation to ascend higher up the staircase or stay at the same step. If you are satisfied at your present level of spiritual understanding and growth, the Lord will leave you

there in hopes that you will discover your need. In Song of
Solomon 2:7 he directed other believers to not distract her:

> "O ye Daughters of Jerusalem, by the roes,
> and by the hinds of the field, that ye stir not
> up, nor awake my love, till she please."

The Lord instructs all who were near her to not satisfy this spiritual need in her. He wants her to become discontent so that she will realize her lack and seek Him again. He even distances Himself and hides behind a garden lattice. Song of Solomon 2:9 tells us:

> "My beloved is like a roe or a young hart:
> behold, he standeth behind our wall, he
> looketh forth at the windows, shewing him-
> self through the lattice."

The Shulamite is now awakened to this fact—she missed an opportunity to be with her lover. After tossing and turning upon her bed, she realizes there is nothing more for her to do except to search for Him. She knows now that this is the only remedy. He promised her he wouldn't be far away. He is in fact, closer than she thinks. The Lord, hidden behind a lattice, is partially visible, so that His sleepy bride might take notice of His presence. The wall or lattice that He is behind represents those things that hinder or separate the bride from fully seeing Him. These prejudices or issues that have accumulated in the bride's life cause her to have a "partial blindness" (Rom. 11:25, Lev. 21:20).

How many times have we've missed Him standing on the outside, peering through and desiring to come in? Has your heart become heavy in sleep? Awaken, O daughter of Zion! Seek Him now while He can be found! Ask the Lord to reveal anything to you that may be hindering you from seeing your Heavenly Bridegroom.

# Leaping Upon Mountains

Song of Solomon 2:8 reads, "The voice of my beloved! behold, he cometh leaping upon the mountains, skipping upon the hills." This revelation of His leaping and skipping is to bring her up another step, upon which the experience of His manifest presence will be made available to her.

Here He presents Himself as a conquering warrior-King, literally leaping on the mountains. "Mountains" biblically symbolize "nations or people." He is revealing Himself to her as King of Kings and Lord of Lords over all the earth.

Yeshua has overcome the world in the sense of being the absolute Authority, destined to rule and reign. Yeshua is also overcoming the personal battles in the bride's life. He was tested in all areas of His fleshly life and was victorious. He gives this revelation to the bride: the power is there for you to overcome this world.

Rebecca Park Totilo

This is the essence of the dance—a dance of intimacy which comes from a deep passion for the Heavenly Bridegroom.

Song of Solomon 2:17 says:

"Until the day break, and the shadows flee away, turn, my beloved, and be thou like a roe or a young hart upon the mountains of Bether."

He pleads with her to reconsider. Notice there is a time limit on this challenge—"until the day break." His word to her is to quickly turn with an invitation is to leap the mountaintops.

Bether in Hebrew means "cleft." His intention is not for her to forsake her knowledge of Yeshua as the King who placed her in the cleft of the rock of intimacy. She needs to take this experience with her and move forward. He is letting her know that His manifest presence will always be with her even though she needs to leave that place and venture into uncharted territory.

In Song of Solomon 4:8 we read:

"Come with me from Lebanon, my spouse, with me from Lebanon: look from the top of Amana, from the top of Shenir and Hermon, from the lions' dens, from the mountains of the leopards."

Here the King is exhorting the bride to come that he may take her yet deeper in the Spirit.

Lebanon in Hebrew means "white mountain," symbolizing "purity or spotlessness." It is derived from a word meaning "the heart," and the primary root meaning "to be enclosed." Thus, this place of devotion and purity of heart is hidden for only the King to behold.

There are five mountains that she is to go to with the King, which will require great leaps of faith to accomplish. It is interesting to note that "five" is symbolic of the need of grace.

The first mountain is Amana. In Hebrew, this word means "covenant," derived from a word that means "sure or faithful," and comes from the primary root that means "to build up or foster."

Revelation 7:3 says:

"Hurt not the earth, neither the sea, nor the trees, till we have sealed the servants of our God in their foreheads."

Just as God made an everlasting covenant with Abraham, He is now seeking a covenant people. In the same way the covenant with Abraham was made by circumcision (sealing of the covenant), these who press through the veil will also be sealed. They are sealed in their foreheads—a circumcision in the foreskin of the mind.

Romans 2:29 says:

"But he is a Jew, which is one inwardly; and circumcision is that of the heart, in the spirit, and not in the letter; whose praise is not of men, but of God."

And Hebrews 10:16 tells us:

"This is the covenant that I will make with them after those days, saith the Lord, I will put my laws into their hearts, and in their minds will I write them."

The second mountain is Shenir, which in Hebrew means "peak or Heavenly realm." Rabbi Sha'ul said in his letter to the Ephesians, "Blessed be the God and Father of our Lord Jesus Christ, who hath blessed us with all spiritual blessings in heavenly places in Christ" (Eph. 1:3).

This peak is to dwell permanently in the Heavenly places, or realm. It is there where the spiritual blessings reside and the maturing bride is invited to dwell.

The third mountain is called Hermon. In Hebrew this means "abrupt," and is also derived from a word meaning "to devote, seclude, or be blunt."

There will be abrupt change in the spiritual climate that many will miss if they are not abiding in the Spirit. The anointing will also bring sudden change upon whom it rests. It will require faith to run after and be fully devoted to follow after this abrupt change, and grace to rest in the next level.

The fourth mountain is one of "lions' dens," and in Hebrew this word means "to gather or to plunk from violence."

It will be from this mountain that the harvest will be gathered and the land taken. Matthew 11:12 says, "And from the days of John the Baptist until now the kingdom of heaven suffereth violence, and the violent take it by force." It will be by force that we take the land. We need to be courageous!

The fifth mountain is one of "leopards," and in Hebrew this word means "limpid or transparent clearness."

This last mountain symbolizes the level of purity that the King is looking to take us to. "Transparent" means we no longer have any hidden sin in our lives. We stand before the Father and Man with a clear conscience. Those upon this mountain have been purged from dead works by the blood of Christ and press forward to serve the living God without religious form.

The five mountains:

- Amana (covenant)
- Shenir (abiding or dwelling place)

The Lord of the Dance

- Hermon (abrupt change)
- Lions' Dens (violence or courage)
- Leopards (transparent or clear conscience)

# Dance of Embrace

Naturally, we express our faith through our moves in worship to Him, but there is something much more He desires: to express Himself in us through the dance.

John 1:1, 14a declares, "In the beginning was the Word, and the Word was with God, and the Word was God. And the Word was made flesh, and dwelt among us." He became the Word with skin on. We too, must allow the Word to be made flesh in our dance.

Through each dance step, God is faithfully revealing how to overcome and have victory in every area of your life. In this dance, we learn our deliverance and provision is only in Him. This is when all natural provision is gone and we have no provision of our own.

This part of the dance is when you see God slide his foot back and swoop you down in his embrace, allowing Him to take the lead.

Song of Solomon 2:6 says, "His left hand is under my head, and his right hand doth embrace me."

The Hebrew word for "left" is *Samo'wl*, which means "left or by implication north." North biblically is indicative of "judgment or correction." Correction came to Israel from the North. His hand of correction is under her head because it is her mind that is about to be renewed by the infilling of the Holy Spirit.

Romans 12:2 tells us, "And be not conformed to this world; but be ye transformed by the renewing of your mind, that ye may prove what is that good, and acceptable, and perfect, will of God."

The Hebrew word for "right" is *Yamiyn*, which means "right or by implication south." South biblically symbolizes "mercy." Abram went south when the famine came upon the land, as well as Jacob. Egypt is south, and represents protection and provision. It is only for a season He expects Israel to stay in Egypt; their inheritance is in the promised-land.

His right hand of mercy and goodness embraced her. His mercy and grace is what will carry us through trials and tribulations. His mercy and goodness confirms His love to us. The bride needs both.

With His left hand He comforts us and with His right hand He corrects us.

# *Voice of My Beloved*

Song of Solomon 5:2 says, "I sleep, but my heart waketh: it is the voice of my beloved that knocketh, saying, Open to me, my sister, my love, my dove, my undefiled: for my head is filled with dew, and my locks with the drops of the night."

The Bride awakens to the voice of her beloved. He has returned and stands at her door knocking. The words of Yeshua from Revelation 3:10 come alive with a fuller, richer meaning when coupled with the prophetic words of Solomon:

> "Behold, I stand at the door, and knock: if any man hear my voice, and open the door, I will come in to him, and will sup with him, and he with me."

The Groom returns from the garden with his hair wet from dew, where He prostrated himself upon worn knees before the Father praying for His beloved Bride, Israel. His time of suffering was now finished—He had conquered death on the tree.

The Shulamite hesitated in answering the door. She had removed her fuzzy pink slippers and robe and was now curled up in bed comfortable with her favorite novel. After making excuses she decided to open the door.

Song of Solomon 5:5 says, "I rose up to open to my beloved, and my hands dropped with myrrh, my fingers with sweet smelling myrrh, upon the handles of the lock."

Because of her delay in answering the door, her lover is no longer there. She does, however, receive his anointing of Myrrh that he left on the doorknob.

The Hebrew word for "myrrh" is *Mowr*, and its root word is *Marar*, which means "bitterness." Myrrh is symbolic of death, as it was a fragrance used for embalming and preparing bodies for burial. In the Middle East, women take a bundle of myrrh and wear it around their necks at night in preparation of a future wedding (SS 1:13). Esther also had six months treatment with the oil of myrrh in preparation for the King.

Myrrh is extracted from a tree by piercing the heart-wood, and the resin oozes out into hard, little red droplets called "tears," similar to what Yeshua experienced in the Garden of Gethsemane. She now shares in His sufferings.

He continues in Song of Solomon 4:6b, saying, "I will get me to the mountain of myrrh, and to the hill of frankincense." His time of suffering has passed; He has conquered death and now reigns as King and High Priest. "Frankincense" symbolic of His Kingdom and the intercession of the saints, burns night and day in the throne room, as an offering and a symbol of undying devotion.

# A Company of Banners

He clothes us with authority when we appear as a mighty army, waving banners of truth, declaring His rule over the earth.

He describes the Shulamite in Song of Solomon 6:4-5: "Thou art beautiful, O my love, as Tirzah, comely as Jerusalem, terrible ("awesome") as an army with banners. Turn away thine eyes from me, for they have overcome me."

Tirzah in Hebrew means "favorable." In this love relationship there is favor or grace. As His remnant bride, we have been given His unmerited favor through His agape love.

The Hebrew name for "Jerusalem" is *Yarushalaim*, which means "teaching of peace." Peace only exists on one condition: where there is only one will. Here the bride is declaring to the King that He is her peace, her strong tower, and her fortress. She can find rest and peace in the midst of turmoil. Isaiah 26:3 says, "Thou wilt keep him in perfect peace, whose mind is stayed on thee: because he trusteth in thee."

As an army of dancers or Mechowlah, we are His army and must take our place in ranks. The Shulamite is being entreated as a corporate bride to perform her "dance of Mahanaim," which means two camps (symbolic of the two houses of Israel). The term Mahanaim refers to the camp in which Jacob returned to (the land of his fathers) and an angel met him and said, "This is God's camp." This includes all of the House of Israel and Judah dancing as one: the men danced (Jeremiah 31:13), the women danced (Exodus 15:20) and the children danced (Job 21:11).

The bride's dance will include waving banners. The Hebrew word for "banner" is *Dagal*, which means "to behold or set up a standard (as in battle)."

The dance of the Shulamite is a dance of devotion, a victorious dance over our enemies. He is raising an army that will execute judgment upon His enemies in His name, for the pulling down of strongholds. But it will be a series of events, like the staircase that will teach us as we ascend the steps.

## The Lord of the Dance

In the Hebrew Scriptures we find multiple words translated as "dance." In Exodus 15:20, we see Miriam the prophetess (sister to Moses and Aaron), dance with the other women with timbrels. The Hebrew word used in this reference is *Mekholaw*, which means joy and celebration by dancing. In the book of Psalms we see the Hebrew word *Mawkhole*, referring to a round dance of praise. In 1 Samuel 30:16, there was dancing during the celebration of the feasts of the Lord. The Hebrew word used in this reference is *Khawgag*. In Judges 21:21 the daughters of Shiloh came out to perform their dances. The Hebrew word used in this Scripture for "dance" is *Chuwl*, which means "to twist or whirl in a circular or spiral matter (like a staircase), dance, bear, wait, writhe in pain (as in childbirth), bring forth, drive away, fall grievously in pain, make, rest, be sore, shake, tremble, trust, and be wounded." Interestingly, the Israelites made big crop circles in the wilderness, but at Jericho those same dance steps and circles brought down the walls. In 1 Samuel 6:14 David danced before the Lord with all his might. The Hebrew word *Kawrar* means literally to whirl, to dance. And in 1 Chronicles 15:29, King David danced and played music. In this scripture, the Hebrew word is *Rawkad*, which means to stamp, spring about, dance, jump, leap and skip. In all of these references we can certainly see how important dancing before the Lord is to the King of the Universe.

Your movement will enthrall our Heavenly Bridegroom so much that He will have to turn away, because this dance plays out His purposes and callings. It will be a beautiful choreographed dance, full of creative life with breathtaking motion—it is the dance of all dances, because He is the Lord of the Dance.

# The Stairs of Ascent

In the old City of David, there are monumental stairs leading up to the Hulda Gate near the Temple Mount. The staircase uncovered from archaeological digs reveals 15 pairs of alternating sizes of broad-narrow steps. The stairs were constructed in this way so a pilgrim present for the Feast of the Lord could recite the 15 Psalms of Ascent when going up to the Temple Mount to worship. This caused the visitor to look down in humility—bowing in holiness and contemplation with each step they took.

In the article entitled, "The Secret of the Fifteen Steps," Yaakov Paley relates a story of the Priests descent of these stairs during the feast of Sukkot (Tabernacles) for the Water-Drawing Celebration.:

> "The Talmud describes the entire scene which took place every Sukkot at the Holy Temple in Jerusalem with gleaming golden candlesticks, burly oil bearers, dancing rabbis, juggling sages, and a vast rejoicing mass

of Jews. The all-night dancing and rejoicing took place in the large Women's Courtyard of the Temple (the men in the courtyard below, the women on an elaborate balcony that was especially erected for the ceremony), whilst upon the broad circular stairs that led up to the Men's Courtyard, the Levites stood with "harps, lyres, cymbals, trumpets" and many other musical instruments. The Levites provided the musical fanfare and spiritual song that kept Jerusalem wide-eyed till dawn, as they stood upon those "fifteen steps that led down from the Israelites' Courtyard to the Women's Courtyard, that correspond to the fifteen 'Songs of Ascent' 2 (Shir Hamaalot) found in Psalms." At the call of the dawn, two priests sounded their trumpets and began to descend these fifteen steps. They paused on the tenth step to sound their trumpets once more . . ."

Let each step you take on your journey as the Bride of Messiah be one of reverence and holiness. Ponder each verse He gives you, savor each moment in sweet communion together, and live every moment in Him!

# About Rebecca at the Well

Rebecca at the Well Foundation is a non-profit Judeo-Christian organization devoted to inspiring believers to prepare for the return of the Messiah. By informing the "called out ones" the way to walk in the beauty of holiness, it motivates members of the body to be clothed with righteous acts and deeds as the Bride of Messiah.

In an effort to bridge the gap between Judaism and Christianity, Rebecca at The Well Foundation provides workshops and seminars about the Hebraic roots of our faith that binds us together as one. All believers can celebrate Yeshua's return as they learn how to make themselves ready as a pure and holy bride.

Rebecca Park Totilo, founder and president of the Rebecca at The Well Foundation, is currently touring the country, preparing the bride for her Heavenly Bridegroom. She is available to speak at conferences, seminars and retreats. Please contact her at (727) 688-2115 for more information, or if you would like to have her come and share with your group or congregation.

Visit our website at:

www.rebeccaatthewell.org or www.ratw.org

For e-mail correspondence:

becca@RebeccaAtTheWell.org

For snail mail correspondence:

Rebecca At The Well Foundation

PO Box 60044

St. Petersburg, FL 33784

To order additional copies of

*The Lord Of The Dance*

Have your credit card ready and call:

1 – 727 – 688 – 2115

or please visit our website at

www.RATW.org

Other Book & CD Sets:

*A Portrait of the Bride: The Shulamite*

*The Fragrance of the Bride*

*Who Is the Bride?*

*A Portrait of the Bride: Rebekah*

*Notes*

*Notes*

*Notes*

CPSIA information can be obtained
at www.ICGtesting.com
Printed in the USA
BVHW081322120919
558281BV00008B/266/P